John Muir
My Life
with Nature

By Joseph Cornell
Author, *Sharing Nature with Children*

Illustrations by Elizabeth Ann Kelley
and Christopher Canyon

A Sharing Nature with Children Book

Dawn Publications

Dedication
May we all, like John Muir,
feel a spirit of wonder and joy in the natural world. —Joseph Cornell

Library of Congress Cataloging-in-Publication Data
Muir, John, 1838-1914.
  John Muir : my life with nature / [compiled] by Joseph Cornell.
  — 1st ed.
    p. cm.
Summary: A biography of the man known as "father of America's national parks" and an influential conservationist, told in the first person, using Muir's own words.
  ISBN 1-58469-009-7 (pbk.)
  1. Muir, John, 1838-1914—Juvenile literature. 2. Naturalists—United States—Biography—Juvenile literature. 3. Conservationists—United States—Biography—Juvenile literature. [1. Muir, John, 1838-1914. 2. Naturalists. 3. Conservationists.] I. Title: My life with nature.
II. Cornell, Joseph Bharat. III. Title.
  QH31.M9 A3 2000
  333.7'2'092—dc21   00-008827

DAWN Publications
12402 Bitney Springs Road
Nevada City, CA 95959
800-545-7475
Email: nature@DawnPub.com
Website: www.DawnPub.com

Printed in the United States of America

10 9 8 7 6 5
First Edition

Cover design by Elizabeth Ann Kelley
Design and computer production by Andrea Miles

Table of Contents

A Note from the Author

No one brought nature to life like John Muir. His great love for all living things gave him a rare understanding of the natural world. Birds, bears and flowers all revealed their secret lives to him. When Muir spoke of his encounters with wild animals, trees, and mountain storms, his listeners said it felt as if they were there, experiencing the adventure with him. Muir also excelled at sharing nature through his writings. They are deeply beautiful, filled with wonder and joy for nature. It has been said that Muir was the only person who could turn a government report into poetry!

To stay true to the spirit of Muir as clearly and fully as possible, I have told his story as if he were alive, using his own words and colorful expressions as often as possible. I have, however, simplified and condensed his words to make them more accessible to young readers. I have also linked the events of this story to keep a smooth, narrative flow, writing as I hope Muir would have written. It is, after all, his story.

A native of Scotland, Muir today is remembered as the father of America's national parks. Born in 1838, Muir is considered by many to be the most influential conservationist of modern times. His love of nature continues to inspire people everywhere to take up the cause of preservation.

Joseph Cornell
Nevada City, California

Chapter One

Free As The Wind

As a boy I was fond of everything that was wild. And all my life I've grown fonder and fonder of wild places and wild creatures. Fortunately, around my native town of Dunbar, by the stormy North Sea, there was plenty of wildness. My playmates and I were as wild as the land itself. We loved to wander by the sea and through the fields to hear the birds sing. We often would run long races through the countryside, to see who was fastest. Or we'd walk along the seashore and gaze in wonder at the shells and seaweed, eels and crabs. Best of all we liked to watch the winter storm-waves crash against the rocky shore.

In the spring we stood for hours enjoying the singing and soaring of the skylarks. From the grass where the nest was hidden, the male would suddenly rise as if shot up into the air. Hovering at thirty or forty feet, he'd pour down the most delicious melody: sweet, clear and strong. Then he would soar

One of our best playgrounds was the famous old Dunbar Castle. We tried to see who could climb the highest on the crumbling peaks and crags.

higher and higher until lost to sight. To test our eyes, we watched the lark until he was but a faint speck in the sky. "I see him yet!" we would cry, "I see him yet!" Finally he would soar beyond all our sight, although we could still hear his glorious music. Then suddenly stopping, the singer would appear, falling like a bolt straight down to his nest.

A favorite playground of mine was the abandoned Dunbar Castle, which was over a thousand years old. My friends and I would climb its crumbling walls to see how high we could go. If we did something that tested our courage or daring, we called it a "scootcher."

One day when I was about nine, we discovered a way into the dungeons below the castle walls. When we came to a dark, deep pit, the other boys were too afraid to go in. I handed my small candle to a friend and lowered myself over the edge. Carefully I made my way down the rough rock walls. In the blackness I couldn't see the bottom—the hole seemed to go on forever. My friends kept calling, "Are you doon, Johnnie, are you doon!?" But I couldn't answer, because I was concentrating so hard on finding safe handholds and footholds. Finally I reached the bottom and called out, "Aye, I'm doon!" They were greatly relieved, and when I finally climbed up again, they shouted, "Hurrah for Johnnie! This was the greatest scootcher of them all!"

One evening when I was eleven, my father announced to my brother David and me, "Boys, you don't need to learn your lessons tonight, for we're going to America in the morning!" We were thrilled by the news, because we'd been reading about the wonders of the American wilderness in school.

My father, sister Sarah, brother David, and I sailed for the New World. My mother and my four other brothers and sisters would follow later, when we could build a house big enough for us all. During the last part of our journey to the Wisconsin frontier, we traveled by ox-cart. Within a minute of our arrival, David and I were up in a tree beside a blue jay's nest, feasting our eyes on beautiful green eggs. The handsome birds made a

Pure wilderness—how utterly happy it made us! Nature streaming into us, teaching her glorious living lessons.

When we first came to Wisconsin, we lived in this tiny shanty until father could build a house for the whole family. Here is the picture I drew of it.

desperate screaming, as if we were robbers just like them. We left the eggs untouched, wondering how many other nests we might find in the grand sunny woods.

The glorious Wisconsin wilderness made me utterly happy. It was spring and the land was bursting with new flowers and leaves, and singing songbirds. I was thrilled to make the acquaintance of chickadees and nuthatches, red-winged blackbirds, and bobolinks, and of the many plant people like water lilies, wind-flowers, and lady slippers. For a whole year, I played freely in this magnificent wilderness. 🐦

Chapter Two

Backwoods Genius

When *I turned twelve,* my father needed me to help plow the fields. Carving a farm out of the Wisconsin backwoods was hard work, and required everyone's help. I could hardly hold the plow handles, but I was determined to do as much work as a man could. When I wasn't plowing, I hauled wood, cleared the fields, and cut fence posts. The days were long, and the work was hard. I worked every day, often sixteen hours a day, because there were no schools nearby. Even so, I had a tremendous hunger for knowledge. I loved to read, and I wanted to learn about everything.

In my precious free moments, I read poetry and learned about mathematics. People said I was a genius at making things out of wood and simple materials. I built thermometers, clocks, and a self-setting sawmill. One of my favorites was a contraption I called an "early-rising machine." It was a bed that worked like an alarm clock. When it was time to get up, the bed would rise and tip you out on the floor! Later, I invented a "scholar's desk." This machine selected a book, opened it for you, and after a chosen amount of time, it returned the book to the shelf, then it would bring down the next book!

People were impressed by my inventions, and my neighbors encouraged me to display them at the Wisconsin State Fair in Madison. I was 22 when I left my frontier home, and with fifteen dollars in my pocket, made my way to Madison and a new life in the world.

I immediately became famous at the State Fair. Crowds packed around my machines like swarms of bees. All this attention was a little overwhelming. The newspapers said I was a "genuine genius," but I was afraid to read the stories—my father had always warned me to avoid praise, for fear of vanity—so I just quickly glanced at the headlines then immediately turned away.

Genuine Genius

MADISON — Marquette County inventor John Muir stirred up a flurry at the fairgrounds Temple of Art building with his remarkable "Early Rising Machine." Mesmerized crowds gathered day after day for Mr. Muir's enthusiastic demonstrations and oration. The young wizard's washboard thermometer repeatedly showed amazingly accurate sensiti... Such creativity in material innovation in design

In 1860 I began my studies at the University of Wisconsin. After taking botany, I began studying and collecting flowers wherever I went.

People encouraged me to follow my dream of going to college, and after a year of working odd jobs, I was finally able to go to the University of Wisconsin. I especially enjoyed chemistry, geology, and botany. But I was interested in all the sciences, because they helped me understand nature and the laws God uses to create this physical world.

After taking botany, I began studying and collecting flowers wherever I went. On a ramble one day, I discovered a tiny gem of a lake hidden deep in the forest, surrounded by ferns and oaks. I asked the owner to keep it wild, and I am happy to say that he did this for as long as he owned the farm. This is how I first began to think about preserving wild land in its natural state.

I dreamed of going to South America like the famous explorer Alexander Von Humboldt, to see the plants in the Amazon. At this time, though, I still enjoyed inventing machines, and I liked the rush and roar of factories. Then one night, something happened that helped me choose nature and beauty. I was working in a factory, adjusting a new belt on a pulley with a file, when the file slipped, flew up and pierced the edge of my right eye. My left eye went blind, too, by nerve shock, leaving me in total darkness. I cried out, "My eyes are gone, closed forever on all God's beauty!"

The doctor said I would never see again. In despair I wrote to my friends, "The sunshine and the winds are playing in all the gardens of God, but I—I am lost!" Fortunately, a friend asked an eye specialist to see me, and he said I would be able to see again in time. I stayed in a dark room for many days. Finally, after four weeks, on a cloudy day, I was able to open my eyes outside for the first time. I vowed then that I would devote my life only to the inventions of God. ❦

Chapter Three

Only Wild Beauty

I *couldn't get enough* of wild beauty, so I decided to walk a thousand miles from Indiana to the Gulf of Mexico, studying nature all along the way. I went by the wildest and least traveled way I could find. In Tennessee I saw my first mountains, and in Georgia, new flower companions greeted me everywhere. The sky changed, and I could detect strange sounds in the winds. But in Florida I found the greatest change of all. I was delighted, astonished, and gazed in wonder as if I had fallen upon another star.

In the Cumberland Mountains, a young horseman robbed me, but was sorely disappointed. When he looked in my pack, he found only a comb, brush, towel, soap, underclothing, and a couple of books, so he gave it all back! I had been warned not to take this journey, because the Civil War had just ended and there were many guerrilla bands preying on lonely wanderers. But I had no fear, because I had so little to lose. Nobody was likely to think it worthwhile to rob me, and anyhow, I always had good luck.

All the world was before me and every day was a holiday, so it did not seem important to which of the world's wildernesses I first should wander.

When I reached Savannah, Georgia I had only twenty-five cents left. I had arranged with my brother to send me some of my savings from time to time. My expected money packet hadn't yet arrived, however. So I stretched my money by eating only crackers. While I waited, I built a small hut to live in. I used four bushes as corner posts and tied little branches across the top to support a roof of rushes. I spread a thick mattress of moss over the floor for my bed. My home was so small that I could have picked it up and walked away with it!

Staying outside of town, my only neighbors were oak trees, squirrels, and birds. After discovering my "nest," the little birds woke me up everyday. Instead of happily singing their morning songs, they flew within a few feet of the hut and looked in at

INDIANA

Indianapolis

WEST VIRGINIA

Jeffersonville • Louisville

KENTUCKY

VIRGINIA

Elizabethtown
Munfordville
Glasgow • Glasgow
Junction • Burkesville

Jamestown
Montgomery

NORTH CAROLINA

Kingston • Philadelphia

TENNESSEE

Madisonville • Murphy

Blairsville
Gainesville

SOUTH CAROLINA

ALABAMA

Athens
Thomson • Augusta

GEORGIA

Savannah

Fernandina

Gainesville
Cedar Keys

To Cuba

me through the leaves, then chattered and scolded in half-angry, half-wondering tones. Thus we began to get acquainted. After they learned that I meant them no ill will, they scolded less and sang more.

After a week my money arrived and I continued my journey to Florida. But I caught malaria there, so instead of sailing to South America I sailed for San Francisco, California. I had read of Yosemite Valley and hoped that the cool mountain climate would cure me.

Excited to arrive on the wild side of the continent, I immediately left San Francisco for Yosemite. It was the spring of 1868 when I saw for the first time the great Central Valley of California and the glorious Sierra Nevada Mountains. It was one of the most magnificent sights I've ever beheld: the valley was a vast, flowery sea of color; like a lake of pure sunshine 40 to 50 miles wide and 500 miles long. Behind the valley rose the majestic Sierras, miles high and so radiant they seemed to be made of light, like the wall of some celestial city. Ever since then, I've called these mountains "The Range of Light."

I made my way quickly toward Yosemite, where I discovered that nature had gathered her choicest treasures. Yosemite Valley is about seven miles long, a half-mile to a mile wide, and nearly a mile deep. Every rock in its walls seems to glow with life, while the crystal Merced, the "river of mercy," peacefully glides through its meadows. When I first saw Bridal Veil Fall, my first Yosemite landmark, I remarked to my companion, "See that dainty little fall? It looks small from here, only about 15 or 20 feet high, but it may be 60 or 70." The grand scale of Yosemite had fooled me—that "dainty fall" was really 620 feet high! ❦

Yosemite Valley is about seven miles long, a half-mile to a mile wide, and first saw Bridal Veil Fall—my first Yosemite landmark—I remarked to about 15 or 20 feet high, but it may be 60 or 70." The grand scale of

nearly a mile deep. Every rock in its walls seems to glow with life. When I
my companion, "See that dainty little fall? It looks small from here, only
Yosemite had fooled me—that "dainty fall" was really 620 feet high!

Chapter Four

Favorite Animals

I took a job supervising a shepherd to earn money to help my sisters go to school. This job gave me lots of free time to wander in the mountains. It was my companion Carlo, a Saint Bernard dog, who introduced me to my first Sierra bear. A hunter had trained Carlo, and he knew the scents of all the animals. One day when we were exploring, Carlo ran ahead of me. Down went his tail and knowing nose, smelling something. "Ha, what's this? A bear, I guess," he seemed to say. Carlo turned and looked at me, his intelligent eyes saying, "Yes, it's a bear—come and I will show you." When Carlo knew the bear was very near, he began to walk behind me. I sneaked up to a large tree and slowly looked around it. There, a stone's throw away, stood a 500-pound bear, sniffing the air.

I had been told that black bears would run away from "bad brother man" unless they were wounded or protecting their young. I wanted to see how it ran, so I made a sudden rush toward it, shouting and waving my hat. But the bear didn't run— instead, it stood its ground, ready to fight! Now I wanted to run, but I was afraid the bear might run after me. Just then I remembered another bit of outdoor wisdom: that the power of the human gaze is stronger than that of any animal. So I stared hard at the angry bear, but evidently the bear hadn't learned this wisdom either, because it glared right back. The interview lasted an awfully long time. Finally, neither fearing nor trusting me, it turned and ambled off, looking back now and then to make sure I wasn't following.

To my embarrassment, I realized that the bear had behaved far better than I had. One should never run up to and crowd any wild animal, especially bears! Ever since then, I have tried to give my shaggy-haired neighbors a respectful notice of my approach, and they usually have kept well out of my way. God bless the Yosemite bears! How

In my first interview with a Sierra bear we were frightened and embarrassed, both of us, but the bear's behavior was better than mine.

grandly they blend with their native mountains. No other animal seems as well looked-after by the Sierra wilderness. To him, almost anything is food except granite.

Another of my Sierra favorites is the ouzel, or "water dipper." This joyous, lovable little bird is dressed in a waterproof suit of bluish gray. He usually lives in and around rushing water, and as long as the water sings, so must he. No canyon is too cold for this little fellow, no place too lonely, provided it be rich with falling water. However dark, snowy, blowing, or cloudy the weather, he sings all the same—never with a note of sadness. Once during a severe storm, I saw most of the Yosemite Valley birds cowering out of reach of the snow, their every gesture reflecting storm-weariness and not one cheerful note coming from their bills. Meanwhile, the ouzel displayed his irrepressible gladness; a true mountaineer is he! Go see him and love him, and through him, as through a window, look into Nature's warm heart.

Sierra travelers often complain about seeing few animals. "Trees," they say, "are fine, but where are the animals and birds? We haven't heard a song all day." And it's no wonder! They go in such large groups, make a great noise and dress in such out-landish colors—no wonder animals avoid them. Even the fright-ened pines would run away if they could. But nature-lovers, silent and open-eyed, looking and listening with love, find that animals come to them gladly.

One Sierra morning as I was eating breakfast in a small meadow surrounded by brush, I noticed a deer gazing at me. I kept still, and the deer came forward a step, then paused, snort-ed and quickly fled. But in a few minutes she returned, bring-

ing along two friends. Staying for just a moment, they took off, too. But their curiosity brought them back once more—now with a fourth companion. This time, the deer were satisfied that I meant them no harm, and they settled down in the meadow and ate breakfast with me, just like tame, gentle sheep around a shepherd.

Another time, a whole troop of mountain quail visited me. They are our most handsome and largest quail. Small and stocky, they have a beautiful head plume, which they wear jauntily backwards like a feather in a boy's cap. These ground-dwelling birds are most secretive, and usually run from any threat, flying only if necessary. They wander the lonely mountains in family flocks of six to twenty, living high in the Sierras. Only in winter do they come down to the brushy foothills, but like every true mountaineer, they are quick to follow spring back up into the higher mountains.

I was sitting at the foot of a tree, sketching, when I heard a flock up the valley behind me. Their voices grew increasingly louder, and I knew that they were feeding toward me. I kept very still, hoping to see them, and soon one came within three or four feet, not noticing me any more than if I were a stump or a tree. Along came another, and another, and I was thrilled to get so near a view of these handsome fellows so that I could observe their manners, and hear their low, peaceful notes.

One of them finally saw me. He gazed for a moment in silent wonder, then uttered a strange cry, which was followed immediately by hurried muttered notes that sounded like speech. The others saw me as soon as the alarm was sounded, and they

joined in the wonder talk, gazing and chattering, astonished but not frightened. Then all together they ran back with the news to the rest of the flock. "What is it, what is it? Oh, you never saw the like," they seemed to be saying. "Where? Where?" "Down there by that tree." They approached cautiously, coming past the tree and stretching their necks, looking up in turn as if knowing from the story told them just where I sat. For fifteen or twenty minutes they kept coming and going, venturing within a few feet of me and discussing the wonder in charming chatter. Their curiosity at last satisfied, they began to scatter and feed again, returning in the direction they had come. Sorry to see them go, I followed them as quietly as I could, crawling beneath the bushes and keeping them in sight for an hour or two, learning their habits and finding out what seeds and berries they liked best.🐦

Chapter Five

Forever a Mountaineer

I never took much time to prepare for a trip—just long enough to throw bread and tea in an old sack and jump over the back fence. My pack was as light as a squirrel's tail. Besides bread and tea, I sometimes carried a light blanket, a hat, and a change of underwear. If I didn't have a coat or blanket, I'd warm myself by a small fire and burrow beneath the pine needles at night. A month's worth of supplies cost me only three dollars.

My bread was so hard, I had to throw it against a rock to break it, then soak the pieces in water. Often, I'd be so excited to start a day's adventures that I wouldn't even boil my tea water in the morning; instead, I'd stuff my mouth with tea leaves and pour the water in. It tasted pretty good, if you had a mind to think so. I camped wherever night found me, and when the weather turned bad, my secret of staying warm was to gaze at the wonder of the beautiful scene before me. Sometimes weary, with only animals to compare notes with, I rested beneath spicy pines or on the plushy sod of glacial meadows.

The mountains are calling me and I must go. I drew this of myself climbing the Matterhorn in the High Sierra.

My method of study was to drift from rock to rock and grove to grove. I'd sit for hours watching the birds or squirrels, or looking into the faces of flowers. When I discovered a new plant, I sat beside it for a minute or a day, to make its acquaintance and try to hear what it had to tell me. I asked the boulders where they came from and where they were going. And when I discovered a mountain, I climbed about it and compared it with its neighbors. It's astonishing how high and far we can climb in the mountains we love, and how little we require for food and clothing.

In 1874, I walked from Redding, California to Mt. Shasta, a majestic, snow-covered volcano that rises 10,000 feet above the

If I didn't have a coat or blanket, I'd warm myself by a small fire and burrow beneath the pine needles at night. A month's worth of supplies cost me only three dollars.

surrounding countryside. It was late autumn, and heavy snow blanketed the mountain. I set out at 2 a.m., hoping to reach the summit before an approaching storm. In places, I had to wade through snow as deep as my armpits, and the slope was steep, so my progress was slow. But the bracing air and the sublime beauty of the snowy expanse thrilled my every nerve, making exhaustion impossible. By 10:30 a.m. I had gained the summit.

Returning at dusk, I hollowed out a space behind a big block of lava and immediately fell asleep. When I awoke the next morning, storm clouds covered the sky. I quickly gathered as much wood as possible and staked down my blankets to pre-

Here is my self-portrait. Someone looking at me would see two eyes, like small open spots on a hillside of overgrown and shaggy brush.

vent them from being blown away. The precious bread sack was positioned safely as a pillow, and when the first flakes fell I was ready to welcome them.

Day after day the storm continued, piling snow in weariless abundance. Several times, when the storm ceased for a few minutes, I had the company of a frisky Douglas squirrel. Once a large flock of mountain sheep took shelter near my little nest. Happy and content, I spent my time examining snow crystals and watching snow flakes and dwarf pines dancing together in the wind. The storm lasted about a week, but before it ended I was "rescued." The news had spread that there was a man on the mountain, and that surely he must have perished, but I was as safe as anyone in the lowlands, lying like a squirrel in my warm, fluffy nest and wishing only to be left alone.

The following April, I spent a much more perilous night on Mt. Shasta, trapped by a violent storm at 14,000 feet. The thermometer fell 22° within minutes, then quickly dropped below zero. Hail gave way to snow, and darkness came while the wind rose to the highest pitch of violence and boomed and surged amid the desolate crags, and lightning-flashes cut the gloomy darkness.

My companion, Jerome Fay, and I made a dash for the "hot springs" just below the summit. These steam vents spew out hot smoke and gases from the volcano. "Here," Jerome said, as we shivered in the midst of hissing, sputtering fumaroles, "if we lie down we shall be safe from frost." The heat became unbearable on spots where scalding steam escaped directly through the sludge, and we tried to stop it with snow and mud. The hot spring's deadly carbonic gas would kill us if we fell asleep, so all through the night we called feebly to each other, "Are you awake?" Two feet of snow fell in just a few hours, freezing into a stiff, crusty heap as the temperature fell, adding to our misery. Frozen, blistered, hungry and numb, our bodies seemed lost to us at times. Scalded beneath and freezing above, we made the best of it, for it was our only hope. Finally, the sky cleared and we gazed at the stars, blessed immortals of light shining with marvelous brightness. The star clouds of the Milky Way seemed especially close and I delighted in their radiance and tranquility.

The frost, however, grew ever more intense, until we were covered over with ice and crusty snow. After thirteen hours— every hour seemed like a year—day began to return. We didn't know if we could walk back to camp, because we had lain all this time without once rising to our feet. But mountaineers always seem to discover reserves of power after a period of deep exhaustion. It's a kind of second life, available only in emergencies like this. I had no great fear that either of us would fail, though one of my arms was already numb and hung useless.

We arose and began our homeward struggle. Our frozen trousers could scarcely be bent at the knee, and we waded

When I first saw Shasta I was alone, afoot and weary. But my blood turned to wine, and I have not been weary since.

through the snow with difficulty. Eventually, we reached the long, final, homeward slopes where we made rapid progress by sliding, shuffling, and pitching headlong down the icy mountain. At 10 a.m. we had reached the trees and knew we were safe; half an hour later, we heard our friend Sisson shouting for us. He had brought horses to carry us home.

Another time, I spent a more enjoyable, glorious storm-day near Yuba Pass. When the wind began to blow, I went outside at once to enjoy it. The pine trees were in ecstasy, and I longed to join them. Young sugar pines were bowing almost to the ground, while grand old trees waved solemnly above them. For hours, I heard the thunderous crack of trees falling—about one tree every two or three minutes. I could also clearly hear the different tones of the trees: closing my eyes, I could effortlessly identify the special music of pine, fir, and oak. Each tree sang its own song and danced its own dance.

Toward mid-day, I reached the summit of the highest ridge, where I thought to climb to the top of a tree to observe the storm and hear the tree's glorious music. In a stand of trees growing closely together I carefully selected the tallest Douglas fir, about 100 feet high, its lithe brushy top rocking and swirling wildly in the blasting gale. I had never enjoyed such thrilling motion. I held on like a bird on a reed while the tree flapped and swished and swirled back and forth. I remained in my lofty perch for hours, enjoying the wild wind-music and feasting on the delicious forest fragrances streaming past me.

I finally came down from the mountains and married when I was 42 years old. All my friends sighed with relief and said "At last!" My wife, Louie, and I lived on her family's ranch in Martinez near San Francisco, and soon we had two daughters, Wanda and Helen. I enjoyed telling them funny stories and taking them on walks in the hills. As soon as Wanda could speak, I taught her the names of the flowers. "For how would you like it," I asked her, "if people didn't call you by your name?" I was

(Left)
Louie Strentzel
Muir, my wife
(Below) Wanda
and Helen Muir,
my two children

a proud papa when years later Wanda and Helen accompanied me on my trips to the Sierra.

For ten years I tended our orchards and vineyards. During that time I was able to earn money to provide for my family's future. But seeing that I was working too hard, Louie sold part of the ranch to give me the freedom to pursue my mountain studies again. I would leave in late summer and return just before the harvest. Later we hired a foreman so I could devote myself completely to my nature work. Louie's concern and loving support is something that I've always treasured. 🐾

Chapter Six

Snow Flowers, Ice Rivers and a Dog

I've always been fascinated by glaciers. Soon after arriving in California, I discovered that glaciers still live in the Sierras, although barely surviving high in the mountains. Most people believed they were just snowfields, but I realized that they were true glaciers, though reduced to a tiny fraction of their former giant size. I could tell that in times past, when the Earth's climate was cooler, these rivers of ice had been much larger, and that they had carved the Sierras and Yosemite.

Glaciers are born of fallen snowflakes compressed into ice. Their weight causes them to flow downhill, like very slow rivers. The tiny, fragile snow flowers, flying through darkened skies, seem to take counsel and say, "Come, let us help one another. We are many, and together we will be strong. Let us march together and roll away the stones from the mountains and set the landscape free."

I had heard that there were huge glaciers in Southeast Alaska, still carving noble, newborn scenery, so in 1879 I went to Alaska for the first time. Just 12 years before, the United

Here is my sketch of a living glacier I discovered high in the Yosemite mountains. One learns that the world, though made, is yet being made—that this is still the morning of creation.

States had purchased Alaska from Russia. We traveled by canoe for hundreds of miles among the islands that protected the coast. My friend, the missionary S. Hall Young, and I had lots of adventures, and some narrow escapes.

At the end of our trip, we discovered a long bay that was filled with icebergs. No one had ever explored this region before. The inlet, which was surrounded by big icy mountains, is now called Glacier Bay. But when Captain George Vancouver sailed past this part of the coast in 1794, the bay didn't even exist, because the inlet was completely choked with glacier ice over 4000 feet high, 20 miles wide, and 100 miles long. When we

When I viewed Glacier Bay for the first time, I saw icebergs floating

arrived just 85 years later, the glacier had retreated 48 miles up the inlet!

It was near here, on a return trip the following summer, that a little dog and I had an exciting adventure that changed our lives. Reverend Young brought along his dog, Stickeen. "The trip is too hard for such a helpless, little creature," I told Young. But he assured me that Stickeen would be no trouble at all. "He's a perfect wonder of a dog. He can endure cold like a bear, swim like a seal, and is very wise and cunning." Young gave Stickeen so much praise that it seemed to me he might be the most interesting member of our party.

rywhere and five huge glaciers.

Stickeen had long, silky black hair, short legs, and a showy tail like a squirrel's. He was always quiet, and never showed any visible enthusiasm—he seemed as cold and unfeeling as a glacier. Stickeen was his own dog, and he always insisted on having his way. But this little philosopher loved adventure, and he began to follow me wherever I went.

One day, Stickeen and I left camp early to explore a glacier. It was wild and stormy as we crossed the seven-mile width of the ice river, then followed it into the mountains. Our path was frequently blocked by huge crevasses—cracks in the ice, some of them a thousand feet deep, and more than eight feet across.

Glaciers are born of fallen
snowflakes compressed into ice.
Their weight causes them to flow
downhill, like very slow rivers.

I would carefully examine the smaller cracks, then jump over, while Stickeen sailed over them like a flying cloud. His total lack of concern worried me, and I warned him to be careful.

Late in the day, we were rapidly descending the glacier as the falling sun and the storm-darkness urged us homeward. We ran as much as we could, and we crossed the glacier further upstream where the ice seemed smooth. We were making good progress until we came to a maze of crevasses and jumbled ice. For every 100 yards of advance, we had to walk a mile back and forth, looking for safe ground. Again and again I was sorely tested by the wide crevasses that I had to jump over. Stickeen followed easily, trotting along as if the glacier were a playground. He showed no trace of fear, and seemed ready for anything, although I noticed that he kept close to me.

Eventually, our way was blocked by a great crevasse. I knew I could never jump back over a large crack we had just crossed, because its far bank was too high, so we were trapped on an island of ice, two miles long and several hundred yards wide! There was only one way off our ice island, a narrow bridge of ice that ran 70 feet to the other side. Low in the middle from melting, it was 10 feet down just to get to the bridge, and another 10 feet up on the other side. The cold, wet weather, howling wind, and failing light made it even more dangerous. This ice bridge was so frightening that when I saw it, I quickly dismissed it from my mind. Finally, though, realizing that it was our only chance, I knew we'd have to try it. After studying the route for a long time, I felt that it just might be possible.

I carefully cut steps down to the bridge, then crossed over to the far side. Now came the hardest part. As I cut a ladder of steps up the cliff, I was forced to chip and climb, then hold on with my feet and fingers crammed into tiny notches in the ice. I had never been under such deadly strain. How I got up the cliff, I could never tell you. The feat seemed to have been done by someone else.

But what of Stickeen, our brave mountaineer! As soon as he realized that I was going across, he peered into the chasm then looked at me plaintively and began to mutter and whine, saying just as plainly as if with words, "Surely you aren't going into that awful place!" I was proud of Stickeen, because never before had he recognized that ice was slippery and dangerous. To calm him, I said, "Hush your fears, my boy, we'll get across, though it won't be easy. We must risk our lives to save them." Stickeen, unconvinced, ran off to find another way. Of course he failed, and when he returned, he began to cry even more mournfully as I started across the bridge, "O-o-oh! What a place! No-o-o, I can never go-o-o down there!"

When I made it to the other side, Stickeen moaned with even greater despair. Realizing that he had no choice, he steadied himself and began his attempt. He slid his front feet forward and carefully secured them on the first step. Then he brought his back feet down ever so slowly until all four feet were bunched onto one step. This left him teetering on the sheer ice wall. In this way, Stickeen descended the cliff until he had reached the bridge. Bracing himself against the buffeting wind and placing each step with the utmost care, Stickeen made his way across.

When Stickeen reached the face of the ice cliff, I was worried, because dogs are poor climbers. If Stickeen was destined to fall, I knew this would be the place. As I tried to make a noose with my clothes to haul him up, Stickeen sat very still, his eyes steeled in concentration. Carefully, he looked to see how far apart the steps were. Then, in a wild rush, Stickeen bounded upward and caught the first step, then the second, the third, fourth, and on and on until he shot up over the cliff to safety.

Stickeen's rescue filled him with joy—he flashed and darted here and there, screaming and shouting and swirling around like a leaf in a whirlwind, rolling over and over, then crying and sobbing. When I ran to him, fearing he might die of joy,

This child-dog of the wilderness taught me much. He enlarged my life, and extended its boundaries. Ever since, I have felt a deeper sympathy for all my fellow mortals.

Stickeen ran off 200 or 300 yards in one direction, then turned and raced back and launched himself at my face, nearly knocking me down. All the time, he was screaming: "Saved! Saved! Saved! We made it, John, didn't we!" "Now, now, Stickeen, settle down," I said as I tried to calm him, "we've many miles still to go." The ice ahead contained thousands of crevasses, but they were common ones, and we reached camp safely about 10 o'clock at night.

Afterwards, Stickeen was a changed dog. Our storm-battle brought Stickeen to life. He no longer kept to himself, but tried to keep me constantly in sight. At night, when it was quiet around the campfire, Stickeen would rest his head on my knee and look into my eyes. His seemed to say, "Wasn't that an awful time we had together on the glacier?"

Stickeen enlarged my life and extended its boundaries. This child dog of the wilderness taught me much. I learned that in both humans and animals, love, hope, and fear are essentially the same, and fall on all alike like sunshine. Through him, as through a window, I was able to look into the heart of all my horizontal brothers of the animal world. Ever since, I have felt a deeper sympathy for all my fellow mortals. ❧

Chapter Seven

Make the Mountains Glad

I *have loved the plant* people, too, and I've enjoyed making their acquaintance. Happy is the man to whom every tree is a friend. And so also with the smaller flower people that dwell beneath them. To know them, you must be as free of cares and time as the plants themselves. I have traveled all over the world to observe them in their native homes.

One tree that I've come to know well lives only in California. It's the Sequoia, or Big Tree—the grandest tree of them all. With a mule named Brownie, I once traveled two hundreds miles to see the places where they lived. When I first arrived in Yosemite, I asked a shepherd if the Sequoias were as big as people said. He replied: "Oh, yes sir, you bet. They're whales. I never used to believe half I heard about the awful size of California trees, but they're monsters all right. One of them over here, they tell me, is the biggest tree in the whole world!"

Giant Sequoias are the biggest trees in the world, and the tallest in the Sierra. They can be 30 feet thick and nearly 300 feet

Happy is the man to whom every tree is a friend.

high. They are the first to receive the sun's morning light, and the last to say goodbye. These stately trees never lose their poise, and stay upright and serene even during the mightiest storms. No other tree in the world, as far as I know, has looked down on so many centuries.[1] It's common for them to live for more than 3,000 years. In all my explorations, I've never found a diseased Sequoia. Forest fires seldom harm the older ones, and only a bolt of lightning can end their centuries of life.

Sadly, since settlers discovered them in 1858, these ancient giants have been cut down and blown apart with dynamite to make grape stakes and roof shingles. Once a centuries old Sequoia was felled just to make a dance floor for an evening of fun. And the grandest of all the groves, with the tallest trees, was completely cut down.

1. Bristlecone pines, some living for almost 5,000 years, have since been found to be older than the Giant Sequoias.

Other tree-lovers and I became alarmed at the destruction of our forests and scenic lands. We discovered that 5 to 10 times as much timber was destroyed as was used. During the summer, smoke from sawmills and forest fires was so thick and black that no sunbeam could pierce it. With other botanists, I studied forests all over the United States and wrote a report for our nation's government. The lawmakers ignored our recommendations, so I went directly to the American people. I wrote about our great forests and the harm being done to them, appealing to the American people for their help:

> *Every other civilized nation has had to care for its forests. Yet we have let ours be stolen and wasted at will. Any fool can destroy trees. They cannot defend themselves or run away. And few destroyers of trees ever plant any. Nor can planting restore our vast aboriginal giants. It took more than 3,000 years to make some of the oldest of the Sequoias, trees that are still standing in perfect strength and beauty, waving and singing in the mighty forests of the Sierras. Through wonderful, eventful centuries God has cared for these trees and saved them from drought, disease, and a thousand storms. But He cannot save them from sawmills and fools—this is left to the American people.*

Hearing about this senseless destruction, the American people cried out: "Save what is left of our forests!" Finally, the government started to create preserves to protect our trees. It was a good start, but there was still much more to be done.

In 1892 I helped to establish the Sierra Club to protect nature and persuade people to come and enjoy our western wildlands. I served as president of the Sierra Club for its first 22 years, during which time we helped create the U.S. Forest Service and many national parks like Yosemite, Rainier, and Grand Canyon.

I am at work in my "scribble den" where many of my books were written.

Here I am, on an outing with members of the Sierra Club.
Although I always felt uncomfortable speaking to groups,
amazingly a friend once said of me, "Never was there a naturalist
who could hold his hearers so well, and none had so much to tell."

I never stopped writing books and articles to help the American people learn to love and protect our wonderful natural heritage. I also penned letters and talked with anyone who would listen.

Speaking to formal audiences, though, was something I never got used to. I was persuaded to give my first speech to the Literary Institute of Sacramento. Although the topic was glaciers, my friends said, "If you go, Johnnie, you'll be able to talk about saving trees, too." For further encouragement, my friend, Willie Keith, gave me one of his High Sierra paintings to take along. "Put it on the stage, Johnnie," he said, "When you see it, you'll think you're in the mountains."

The night of the talk was stormy, and I prayed that everyone would stay home. But hundreds of people came anyway, and as

In 1903, I guided President Theodore Roosevelt in Yosemite. The president asked to meet me there and told me, "I don't want anyone with me but you." Like two truant schoolboys, we skipped the festivities organized by dignitaries seeking the president's favor, and went camping for four days.

I got up to speak I was nervous and wished that I were still an unknown nobody living in the mountains. Apologizing to the audience, I said I had never done this before. I told them I was afraid I might fail. They, too, seemed worried I might. Finally, I thought to look at the painting of the Sierra peaks, and when I did, I quickly forgot about myself. In my mind, I was once again high in the mountains. Remembering now what I had come to tell them, my talk became a great success.

Though I never sought fame, I discovered that my nature writings had made me well known. During my first trip to the East Coast, it seemed that almost everybody wanted to talk to me. I met many influential men and women who helped our cause. At the request of President Theodore Roosevelt, he and I went camping for four days in Yosemite, just by ourselves. When I told him about the timber thieves and other spoilers of the forests, he was very sympathetic. Soon after, he set aside over 148 million acres of forestlands. He also established more than 20 new national parks and monuments.

The idea of preserving land for its own sake was new to most people. Many people opposed the idea—those crying the loudest were the ones making the biggest profit off our wild-lands. Others felt that conservation was important only if it was for the benefit of mankind. Even the director of the newly cre-ated Forest Service said, "We are not preserving the forests because they are beautiful or wild or the habitat of wild ani-mals. We are saving them to make sure there is enough timber for human use." My friend Joseph LeConte challenged this view when he wrote in our Sierra Bulletin, "It is true that trees are for human use. But there are aesthetic uses as well as commercial uses—uses for the spiritual wealth of all, as well as for the mate-rial wealth of some." Our public lands are not owned by the greedy few, but by us all. Everybody needs beauty as well as bread, and places where Nature can heal and cheer us.❦

Chapter Eight

Fellow Mortals

We are told that the world was made for man, but our good Earth made many a journey around the heavens before man was made, and whole kingdoms of creatures enjoyed their lives beforehand. Couldn't it be that Nature has made plants and animals, first of all, for their own happiness? How blind we are to the rights to the rest of creation! And how badly we speak against some of our fellow mortals. Though alligators, snakes, etc., may repel us, they are not evil. They dwell happily in the wilds and are part of God's family.

In the Sierra, the only poisonous snakes we have are rattlesnakes. Poor creatures, they are loved only by their Maker. Yet seldom do they harm any one, being timid and bashful in nature. Before I learned to respect rattlesnakes, I killed two. At first I believed that they should be killed wherever found. The first victim I discovered lying between my feet as I was walking through the grass. Thinking I meant mischief, he went into a coil and threatened to strike. He held his ground a few minutes,

Here is my drawing of a little cabin I built in Yosemite. For the sake of music and society, I led a small stream into it. The rippling stream sang in low, sweet tones, making delightful company, especially at night when I was lying awake.

then tried to get away. I didn't let him get far before I killed him. But afterwards, I felt degraded by the killing business, and farther from heaven.

The second killing might also have been avoided, and I have always felt somewhat guilty about it. In Yosemite I diverted a little stream through my cabin—to supply me with water and music. A few frogs came into my home and made merry with the stream—and also one snake. It was a rattlesnake, and I suppose he came to catch the frogs. Our meeting frightened both of us. Besides being scared, the snake seemed to know that he shouldn't be there. I have looked into the eyes of many wild animals and feel sure I sensed his feelings. I did not want to kill him, but I had many visitors, some of them children, and I often came home late at night.

Since then I have seen a hundred or more rattlesnakes in these mountains. But I have never intentionally disturbed them, nor have they disturbed me to any great extent. I once found that I was sharing my camp with a couple of rattlesnakes. Thinking we might get in each other's way, I chose a nearby boulder to sleep on. Another time, while I was on my knees feeding a fire, one glided right under my arm. He was only trying to get away from me, and there was not the slightest danger, because I kept still and let him to go in peace. The only time I felt myself in serious danger was when I was coming out of the Toulumne Canyon. A boulder was blocking my way, so I pulled myself up over it. As I came over the top, I saw a rattlesnake coiled one foot away, ready to strike. My hands had alarmed him, and he was ready for me. But even then he did not strike.

In vain I tried to explain that I only wanted my bread.

One I discovered as I was making my way through a tangle of brush. I parted the branches and threw my bread bag to an open spot. As I was pushing my way through, I saw a young rattlesnake dragging its tail from beneath my bundle. When he saw me, he eyed me angrily and seemed to be asking why I had thrown that stuff on him. He was so small I was tempted to disregard him. But he struck out angrily and I had to approach the opening from the other side. He had been listening, and when I looked through the brush I found him ready to meet me—with a come-in-if-you-dare expression. In vain I tried to explain that

I only wanted my bread. So I went back a ways and kept still for half an hour, and when I came back he was gone.

Snakes, ants, and beetles—we all travel the Milky Way together and share Heaven's blessings. From the dust of the earth the Creator made us, and from the same material he has made every other creature. When one is alone in these mountains, every tree, every flower, every mountain stream seems to feel the presence of the great Creator. ❦

Chapter Nine

Nature's Goodness

My life has been like a glorious walk in one sunny garden. Even when wild storms and other dangers came my way, Nature has always cared for me. I have always been protected, somehow. Once while scaling a cliff high on Mount Ritter, a peak never before climbed, I was suddenly brought to a dead stop. With outstretched arms, I clung to the rock wall, unable to move up or down. Frightened, and frozen with fear, I knew I couldn't hold on for long and would soon fall to my death. My panic lasted only for a moment, however. A new sense of self strengthened me and quieted my trembling muscles. Every crack in the rock became as clear as if looking through a microscope. A wonderful power came over me, and I climbed to the top with ease.

Another time after a heavy snowfall, I wanted to see the mountains in their new white robes. I spent all day climbing to the rim of Yosemite Valley. Most of the way I sank waist deep in the snow—but I continued on, because I love snow. Just before

My days in the wilderness will live with me always. Everything there was so alive and familiar. Whoever gains the blessings of one mountain day is rich forever.

I reached the ridge, an avalanche caught me. To stay on top of it, and avoid being buried by the swooshing snow, I did the backstroke. I was carried 3,000 feet down to the valley floor—in just a minute. Fortunately, my landing was a safe one, without bruise or scar.

God watches over mountaineers, especially when they are trusting and brave. Every cell in creation has its captain that guides it aright—just as a compass needle is shown its way. And so I have always known whether it was safe to continue my explorations. While climbing Mount Whitney at 11 o'clock at night, I heard a voice inside of me, say "Go back!" I felt as if Someone were turning me around and telling me, "Go down the mountain." I obeyed and descended the mountain.

Beauty and science have led me to many wild places and countries. Many times I could have become money-rich, yet time-poor. But I have chosen Wild Beauty. When I was in Argentina looking at trees, a reporter asked me what my occupation was. I told him, "Tramp—I'm seventy-four, and still good at it!" In all my wandering days, I have never met anyone as free as myself. The world's prizes mean nothing to me. Whoever gains the blessings of one mountain day is rich forever.

My days in the wilderness will live with me always. Everything there was so alive and familiar. It's wonderful how Nature is a part of us. The sun shines not on us, but in us. The rivers flow not past but through us. This whole world is our home and everything is our kin. While in the wilderness, the very stones seem talkative and brotherly. One fancies a heart like our own must be beating in every crystal and cell. No wonder when we consider that we all have the same Father and Mother.

I have tried to tell not what I have done, but what Nature has done—a much more important story—in the hopes that

"The sun shines not on us, but in us. The rivers flow not past, but through us." I felt that the Merced, the river which runs through Yosemite, was the most joyful stream born in the Sierra.

you'll go to Nature, yourself, and learn her secret ways. I have also wanted to make the mountains glad. For nature was made not just for us, but for itself and its own happiness, and is the very smile of God. ✾

Explore
More

In this section you can read more about John Muir, do some of his favorite nature activities, and reflect on how his life may be meaningful to you. Just as Muir, who loved to write, carried a journal with him on all of his travels, you may want to write or draw in a journal of your own as you think about the questions in this section.

Note to parents and teachers: To encourage a more dynamic response to the Explore More activities, you may want to read, or refer to, other Muir stories first. For example, you could have your children review the Nature's Goodness chapter, then read *Be True to Yourself.* Another effective combination is to read the Mount Shasta story first, then *Joy in the Midst of Hardship.* Let your imagination go wild, as Muir used to say, and you will find many more harmonious combinations. You can tell the story yourself, have the children read it individually, or have one child read it aloud to others.

Be True To Yourself

Muir's family and friends wanted him to choose a profession—the more socially acceptable, the better. His interest in inventing machinery and wandering through the countryside looking at plants worried his family. He was already in his mid-20s and hadn't yet settled down, and they were afraid he'd become a "no-account" and embarrass them.

During this time, John received lots of "helpful" suggestions on what he should do with his life. His younger brother David told him, "Forget those confounded weeds, John! Marry, and go into business!" True to himself, though, Muir followed his own star. In his journal he wrote, "I will follow my instincts, be myself for good or ill, and see what will be the upshot. As long as I live, I'll hear waterfalls and birds and winds sing. I'll acquaint myself with the glaciers and wild gardens, and get as near the heart of the world as I can." Fortunately for us—and for the Sierra—he remained true to his dream.

As a young man, Muir showed a type of strength that was different than the kind that conquers mountains and crosses glaciers. It was the courage to live his own ideals, even when others didn't understand or value them. Throughout his life, Muir continued to make decisions that kept him true to his life's purpose.

Perhaps the greatest (and shortest) tribute ever given to John Muir was by Reinhold Messner, a German mountaineer. Messner and an American were climbing in the Swiss Alps. The American was surprised to see the Alps so developed, with hotels, villages, and farms dotting the landscape nearly everywhere. He was accustomed to the untouched beauty of the American wilderness, and he asked Messner why the Alps had so many buildings and signs of human activity. With just three words, Messner explained the difference. He said, "You had Muir."

Robert Underwood Johnson, a leading conservationist of Muir's day, spoke of the tremendous influence Muir had on everyone then. He said appreciatively, "Muir's writings and enthusiasm were the chief forces that inspired the conservation movement. All other torches were lighted from his."

John Muir said he lived "only to entice others to look at Nature's loveliness." In your life, what gives you the most satisfaction and meaning? Name the ideals you want to live by and write about them in your journal.

One Large Family

Muir saw everything as alive and with its own special beauty. His love for all living things was the secret of his ability to write beautifully about nature. Choose something from your area that interests you. It can be a plant or an animal or a natural feature. For example, you can pick a bird, flower, mountain, or even something like the wind! Imagine what its life might be like, and tell what you admire about it. Think also about the kinds of experiences it might have had, and what makes it so special. For an example, look at the sketch Muir drew and read the following thoughts that he had about a California tree:

The Sierra juniper is one of the hardiest of all mountaineers. Growing mostly on ridges and rocks, these brave highlanders live for over twenty centuries on sunshine and snow. Thick and sturdy, the wind has as much influence over them as it does over a glacier boulder. A truly wonderful fellow, he seems to last about as long as the granite he stands on. Surely he is the most enduring of all tree mountaineers—never seeming to die a natural death. If protected from accidents, it would perhaps be immortal. I wish I could live like these junipers, on sunshine and snow, and stand beside them for a thousand years. How much I should see, and how delightful it would be!

Joy In The Midst of Hardship

Muir never let cold or wet weather ruin his fun outdoors. When the weather became challenging, Muir said he didn't notice any real discomfort because he was too busy gazing in wonder at the scenery. The following journal entry of Muir's beautifully describes this:

I was as wet as if I had been swimming after crossing raging torrents and fighting my way through the Alaskan jungle. But everything was deliciously fresh, and I found new and old plant friends, and glacier lessons that made everything bright and light. I saw Calypso borealis, one of my little plant darlings, worth any amount of hardship. And the mosses were indescribably beautiful, so fresh, so bright, and so cheery green. In the evening I managed to make a small fire out of wet twigs, got a cup of tea, stripped off my dripping clothing, wrapped myself in a blanket and lay thinking on the gains of the day. I was glad, rich, and almost comfortable.

Describe a time when you made a challenging situation fun by keeping a positive attitude. What happened?

This Whole Wide Beautiful World

M uir felt that the entire planet was his home and he constantly traveled to see it. While he explored California during the 1870s, he described himself as joyously "loose and lost." He loved to travel, and did so even when he was in his 70s, when he journeyed around the world to study trees, glaciers, and mountains. Naturalist John Burroughs said of Muir, "He could not sit in a corner of the landscape as Thoreau did. He must have a continent for his playground." On the map, (next page) follow the routes of Muir's more wide-ranging excursions.

Muir's Longer Journeys:

A. Scotland to Wisconsin: by sailing ship from Glasgow to New York, on to Albany; sailed the Great Lakes via steamer to Milwaukee. (1849)

B. 1,000 Mile Walk, Indiana to Florida (1867)

C. From Florida to San Francisco by ship, by way of Cuba, New York and Panama (1868)

D. Southeast Alaska (1879-1880, 1880, 1896, 1897)

E. Bering Sea, Wrangel Land, Point Barrow (1881)

F. Europe, including England, Scotland, Norway, Switzerland, France, and Italy (1893)

G. Bering Sea, Saint Lawrence Island, and other points in the far north (1899)

H. Finland, Russia, Siberia, Korea, India, Egypt, Australia, New Zealand, Philippines, and China (1903-1904)

I. Brazil, Argentina, Chile, Uruguay, Africa (1911-1912)

John Muir's Journeys

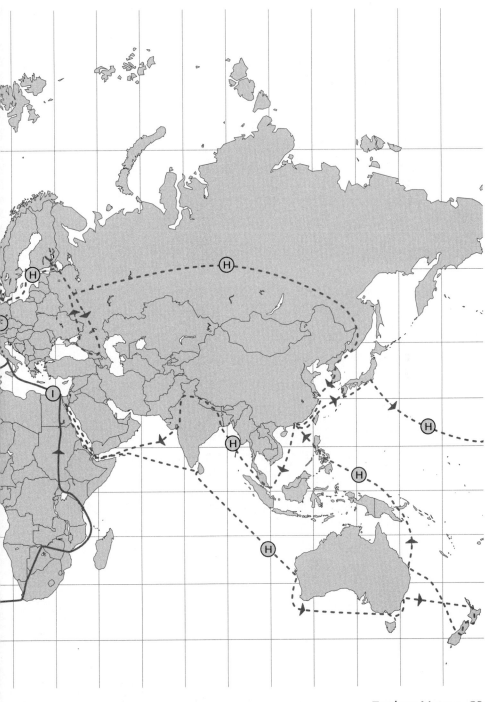

Travel was much slower in Muir's day; for example, his ocean voyage from Scotland to New York took over six weeks by sailing ship. Muir would have been shocked by the speed of travel today. He used to complain that stage-coaches went too fast: "You can't see anything when you're riding twenty miles-per-hour!"

Chronology of John Muir's Life:

1838 – Born in Dunbar, Scotland, April 21st

1849 – Sails to the United States

1860 – Enrolls at University of Wisconsin

1868 – Arrives in California

1871 – First Magazine Article, "The Death of a Glacier," published in the New York Tribune

1880 – Marries Louie Wanda Strentzel

1892 – Founds the Sierra Club and is elected its first President

1903 – Guides President Theodore Roosevelt through Yosemite

1914 – Dies of pneumonia in Los Angles, California, Dec. 24th

True Wealth

Muir said of one of the wealthiest men in the United States, "I am richer than he is, because I have all the money I want—and he doesn't." Several times, Muir could have become quite wealthy. As a young man, he could have made a fortune from his labor-saving factory machines. Later, during the Alaskan Gold Rush, because of his geology training, Muir knew where gold was likely to be found. While camping on Douglas Island, near Juneau, Muir said, "If I were hunting gold, I would stop here." A year later, two rich gold strikes were discovered nearby. For John Muir, though, having enough time for wild beauty, family, and public service was his true wealth. He remarked, "A little money we all need nowadays, but there is nothing about the getting of it that should rob us of our wits."

What does true wealth mean to you? Can you think of ways to simplify your life, so you can have more time for what you value most?

What Is The Secret Of It All?

Muir saw the central principles of all life as harmony and unity. He believed nature evolves less by competition than by cooperation. To make this point, Muir said, "When you try to pick out anything by itself, you find it hitched to everything else in the universe." He noted how the Earth whirls, the winds wander, and the rain falls, all just to feed one humble violet.

Whenever Muir looked at the beautiful symmetry of an island, or the harmony in the colors of flowers, he felt that they were visible signs of a divine intelligence. What do you feel when you're outdoors? What words would you use to describe your experience of nature?

Find a quiet place in nature. In your journal, think about and answer these questions.

John Muir:
Who Was He?

J ohn Muir had a wonderful zest for life, as well as many other exceptional personal qualities. Can you remember a story from his life that matches each of the traits listed below? Make your point by describing what happened to Muir. Then tell how Muir responded to the situation or event, and how he used the quality of courage, will power, or love, etc., to respond in a positive way. (Look through the book again if you wish.)

Courage: Recall a time when Muir was courageous. What do you think made Muir so brave?

Will power: Will power means to meet obstacles or challenges with determination and a high level of energy. Do you think this describes John Muir? Tell about a time when he used his will power, and how it helped him.

Positive Attitude: How did Muir usually react when he found himself in a difficult situation? Was he cheerful and positive, or negative and distrustful? Did he expect the best outcome from a situation, or the worst? Tell about a time when Muir responded to a challenge with a positive attitude.

Love for Others: Did Muir live only for himself, or did he help others? Can you think of a specific time when Muir showed appreciation and concern for his "fellow mortals?"

Discrimination: What were Muir's goals for his life? Were they ones that give true happiness? A successful human being is said to be someone who lives by true principles. Name the principles you feel Muir valued most. The least?

What stories match the following qualities?

   Simplicity   *Inner contentment*   *Love of beauty*

What inspired you most about John Muir's life? What stories of his life did you especially enjoy?

Close To Nature

John Muir wanted others to go out and see nature's loveliness so that they, too, could have the same thrilling experiences. In this activity, you'll have a chance to do some of Muir's favorite activities to help you observe nature better. To begin, look for a place outdoors that feels special to you, one that you enjoy and want to explore.

A. Muir always carried a journal and wrote about the things that interested him. Writing enabled him to share his discoveries with others. He saved his journals and referred to them years later, when he wrote his many books.

When you find your special place, write in your journal some of the first things you notice. Describe any special moments you have in your spot. Examples: seeing an animal, or leaves falling on a crisp autumn day.

B. Muir also regularly drew in his journal. Besides making a record of his observations, drawing helped him see things clearly. Find something you really like and draw it. It can be a tree, rock, or a stunning view of the landscape—whatever you wish. Don't worry about how good your drawing is. It is more important to let your drawing help you observe your subject better and see it in greater detail. What new things did you discover while you were drawing?

C. Muir enjoyed writing and reading poetry. Many people say his written descriptions of nature are so beautiful that they, too, are like poetry. Create your own poem using the following easy-to-use acrostic formula which uses each letter of a word as the beginning of a new line. You will be surprised by how much fun and simple these poems are. Muir did not use this particular form of poetry, but it will help you observe nature closely, as Muir did.

Spend a few minutes watching and enjoying everything around you. Then choose a word that captures the feeling or essence of something you think is especially beautiful. Next, use each letter of the word to begin a line of your poem. For example, while I was walking on Mount Subasio near Assisi, Italy, the flower-covered hillsides conveyed a feeling of excitement as the shadows of the clouds raced over them. I wrote a poem to the word "spring" to express this feeling.

S UN-MADE CLOUD SHADOWS

P LACED ON THE EARTH

R UNNING ACROSS ITS SURFACE

I N AND OUT OF THE SUN I SIT

N OT LONG DOES THE CLOUD'S TWIN STAY

G OING, GOING ON ITS WAY.

Now write the word you have chosen, placing one letter on each line. Then use each letter to begin a line of your poem.

Further Reading

If you'd like to know more about John Muir, I encourage you to read some of the books listed here. They are all excellent.

Two books to begin with:

> *The Wilderness World of John Muir.* This is a compilation of Muir's writings, edited by Edwin Way Teale
>
> *John Muir, Son of the Wilderness.* A biography by Linnie Marsh Wolfe

Books written by John Muir:

> *The Story of my Boyhood and Youth*
> *A Thousand Mile Walk to the Gulf*
> *My First Summer in the Sierra*
> *Mountains of California*
> *The Yosemite*
> *Our National Parks*
> *Travels in Alaska*
> *Stickeen*

Books about John Muir:

> *John Muir and His Legacy,* by Stephen Fox
> *Alaska Days with John Muir,* by Samuel Hall Young

Credits

Illustrations
Elizabeth Ann Kelley: cover, pp 6, 8-9, 12-13, 22, 23, 54, 55
Christopher Canyon: pp 40, 43
Sierra Nevada Natural History, Storer, T. and Usinger, R.L., University of California Press, 1971: pp 24, 25

Photographs
Except as noted below, all photos and drawings are courtesy of the John Muir Papers, Holt-Atherton Department of Special Collections, University of the Pacific Libraries. Copyright 1984 Muir-Hanna Trust.

National Park Service: pp 73, 75

Colby Memorial Library, Sierra Club: pp 46, 50

Robert Frutos: p 32

Quotations
The many quotations from the works of John Muir that appear in this book are taken from the following sources:

Our National Park, John Muir, 1901
Stickeen, John Muir, 1909
My First Summer in the Sierra, John Muir, 1911
The Mountains of California, Century Company, 1911.
The Yosemite, Century Company, 1912.
The Story of My Boyhood and Youth, John Muir 1913
Travels in Alaska, John Muir, 1915
A Thousand Mile Walk, John Muir, 1916
Steep Trails, John Muir, 1918
The Life and Letters of John Muir, William Frederic Bade, 1923
John of the Mountains, Wanda Muir Hanna, ed. Linnie Marsh Wolfe, 1938
Son of the Wilderness, Linnie Marsh Wolfe, Alfred A. Knopf, Inc., 1945; Howard T. Wolfe, 1973
John Muir and His Legacy, Stephen Fox, 1981

To make the text more accessible to young readers, quotations using Muir's words have been simplified and condensed. Because the text is written in the first person, the usual practice of inserting quotation marks has not been observed. Also for ease of reading, the practice of inserting ellipses to represent omissions in the quotations has not been observed.

About the Author

Joseph Cornell is one of the world's leading nature educators. His workshops have been attended by tens of thousands of people around the globe. *Sharing Nature with Children*, the first in the Sharing Nature Series, has sold nearly 500,000 copies and has been translated into more than fifteen languages. He works closely with the Japan Nature Game Association, an organization of over 7,000 educators and leaders using and promoting the Sharing Nature philosophy and activities in Southeast Asia. The founder of *Sharing Nature Worldwide*, Joseph travels frequently to give his programs around the world.

Sharing Nature Foundation

Joseph Cornell and other teachers personally trained by him offer nature awareness workshops throughout the year. These programs draw extensively on the activities and philosophy presented in his six-volume Sharing Nature Series: *Sharing Nature with Children, Sharing Nature with Children II, Journey to the Heart of Nature, John Muir: My Life with Nature, With Beauty Before Me: An Inspirational Guide for Nature Walks,* and *Listening to Nature.*

Every summer Joseph Cornell also conducts a week-long conference retreat in Northern California. Participants experience many ways of deepening their enjoyment of the natural world and come away with effective and inspirational tools they can use both professionally and personally.

Sharing Nature Worldwide is an informal association of organizations and individuals using Cornell's philosophy and activities. To find out more about Sharing Nature coordinators and programs internationally, the *Sharing Nature Journal*, and Cornell's books and his schedule and workshops, please visit the Sharing Nature website at http://www.sharingnature.com. To sponsor a program, or to find out more about the summer conference, contact the Sharing Nature Foundation at 14618 Tyler Foote Road, Nevada City, California 95959; by telephone or fax (530) 478-7650; or online at info@sharingnature.com.

Living Wisdom Schools℠

For many years Joseph Cornell has been part of the Living Wisdom Schools movement which, since 1972, has taught young people through a balanced program of physical, mental, emotional, and spiritual training. In addition to excellence in academics, the curriculum includes those living skills that will enable children to experience true success in life—how to get along with others, how to live in harmony with the Earth, how to concentrate, and how to achieve and maintain inner peace, among other skills. Six broad curriculum areas include self-expression and communication, understanding people, our Earth/our Universe, personal development, cooperation, and wholeness.

To know more about the educational philosophy that has inspired Mr. Cornell's writings and teaching, you may wish to read *Education for Life* by J. Donald Walters (Crystal Clarity Publishers). To learn more about the Living Wisdom philosophy, schools, and teacher training programs write or call Ananda School at 14618 Tyler Foote Road, Nevada City, CA 95959, (530) 478-7640 or visit http://www.efl.org. To know more about the Ananda World Brotherhood Village, an intentional community of which Joseph is a member and which is host to the Living Wisdom Schools, visit its web site at http://www.ananda.org.

Acknowledgments

I would like to gratefully acknowledge the following people for their help, advice, and encouragement: Janene Ford and Daryl Morrison of the Holt-Atherton Dept. of Special Collections for gathering many of the Muir photographs and drawings; George Beinhorn, Frank Helling, Sandy Ross, Nancy Spagnoli, Alan Dyer, Garth Gilchrist, and many Ananda Village friends, for their invaluable suggestions and comments. My special thanks to Anandi for her skillful editing and wonderful enthusiasm for the project.

The Sharing Nature Series by Joseph Cornell

Sharing Nature with Children

The classic parents' and teachers' nature awareness guidebook, now in its second (20th Anniversary) edition.

Sharing Nature with Children II

A sequel to volume one, a treasury of games for all ages, plus a practical handbook for nature educators in which Cornell explains the Flow Learning teaching method. (Formerly titled *Sharing the Joy of Nature.*)

Dawn Publications is dedicated to inspiring in children a deeper understanding and appreciation for all life on Earth. To order, or for a copy of our catalog, please call 800-545-7475, or visit our website at www.dawnpub.com.